TITANS
OF BUSINESS

MARK ZUCKERBERG

Dennis Fertig

Heinemann
LIBRARY

Chicago, Illinois

www.capstonepub.com
Visit our website to find out more information about Heinemann-Raintree books.

To order:

☎ Phone 800-747-4992

 Visit www.capstonepub.com to browse our catalog and order online.

© 2013 Raintree
an imprint of Capstone Global Library, LLC
Chicago, Illinois

Edited by Mark Friedman, Nancy Dickmann, and Claire Throp
Designed by Richard Parker
Picture research by Liz Alexander
Original Illustrations © Capstone Global Library Ltd 2013
Illustrations by Darren Lingard
Originated by Capstone Global Library Ltd
Printed and bound in China by CTPS

16 15 14 13 12
10 9 8 7 6 5 4 3 2 1

Library of Congress Cataloging-in-Publication Data
Fertig, Dennis.
  Mark Zuckerberg / Dennis Fertig.
    p. cm.—(Titans of business)
  Includes bibliographical references and index.
  ISBN 978-1-4329-6426-9 (hb)—ISBN 978-1-4329-6433-7 (pb) 1. Zuckerberg, Mark, 1984- 2. Facebook (Firm) 3. Facebook (Electronic resource) 4. Webmasters—United States—Biography. I. Title.
  HM479.Z83F47 2013
  006.7'54092—dc23   2011050749
  [B]

Acknowledgments
We would like to thank the following for permission to reproduce photographs: Alamy pp. 4 (© Allstar Picture Library), 5 (© Newscast), 13 (© NetPhotos), 20 (© NetPics), 23 (© Keith Morris), 30 (© Richard Levine); Corbis pp. 8 (© Arne Hodalic), 11, 14 (© Rick Friedman), 33 (© Laurent Gillieron/epa), 37 (© Wu Kaixiang/Xinhua Press), 41 (© Christian Liewig/Liewig Media Sports), 43 (© Mike Kepka/San Francisco Chronicle); Getty Images pp. 6 (Paul Morris/Bloomberg), 17 (Juana Arias/The Washington Post); Press Association Images pp. 7 (Paul Sakuma/AP), 9 (Jay LaPrete/NCAA Photos), 27 (Karen T. Borchers/LANDOV), 19 (DPA DEUTSCHE PRESS-AGENTUR/DPA); Press Association Images pp. 21, 39; Rex Features pp. 29 (Sipa Press), 35 (NBCUPHOTOBANK); Shutterstock pp. 12 (© Yevgenia Gorbulsky), 25 (© Benis Arapovic), 31 (© Todd Klassy); The Kobal Collection p. 34 (Columbia Pictures).

Cover photograph reproduced with permission of Corbis/© Kimberly White/Reuters (main image) and Shutterstock/© Eky Studio (background image).

Every effort has been made to contact copyright holders of any material reproduced in this book. Any omissions will be rectified in subsequent printings if notice is given to the publisher.

Disclaimer
All the Internet addresses (URLs) given in this book were valid at the time of going to press. However, due to the dynamic nature of the Internet, some addresses may have changed, or sites may have changed or ceased to exist since publication. While the author and publisher regret any inconvenience this may cause readers, no responsibility for any such changes can be accepted by either the author or the publisher.

Contents

Find out what you need to do to have a successful career like Mark Zuckerberg.

Read what Mark Zuckerberg has said or what has been said about him.

Learn more about the people who influenced Mark Zuckerberg.

Discover more about the industry that Mark Zuckerberg works in.

Words printed in **bold** are explained in the glossary.

The Many Faces of Facebook

In 2002, Mark Zuckerberg was a student at Harvard University in Cambridge, Massachusetts. Like all Harvard students, he was given a printed student **directory**. The booklet listed every student's name, where they lived, and their photos. Students could flip through the directory and figure out who they knew, or who they wanted to know. At Harvard and many other universities, these kinds of directories were called "facebooks."

Old-fashioned

Harvard's facebook seemed old-fashioned to many students. Why was it printed in a book, and not online? Zuckerberg decided to do something about it. In February 2004, he started a website called Thefacebook.com. Harvard students could voluntarily sign up, share some information, and post a good photo of themselves. It seemed like a good idea.

Did Mark Zuckerberg know how successful his idea would really be?

It was a very good idea. By the end of 2011, 845 million people around the world were regularly using his website—only now it was simply called Facebook.

This is just one of the millions of faces on Facebook.

A powerful tool

Every day, people use Facebook to exchange news, photos, and much more. Together they spend 700 billion minutes per month interacting with each other. Facebook has also become a tool that charities use to raise money. Political groups use it to shape world governments. Businesses use Facebook to reach millions of customers.

Thanks to Facebook, Mark Zuckerberg has become the youngest self-made billionaire in history. He could be worth even more when shares in Facebook are sold to the public in 2012.

Zuckerberg is clever, maybe even a genius, but he could not have known that his idea would lead to all of this, could he?

A Child of the Computer Age

Mark Zuckerberg was born in 1984 in White Plains, New York. His father was a dentist known as "Painless Dr. Z." His mother was a psychiatrist. Mark, their only son, was the second of four children.

The Zuckerberg parents were intelligent, well educated, and supportive of their children. Not surprisingly, all four children were intelligent, well educated, and successful. They got along well with each other and often worked on projects together. One project was a film they made called *The Star Wars Sill-ogy*. It poked fun at the real *Star Wars*.

Zuckerberg speaks at a conference in 2011, where he unveils new features for Facebook. He also showed a photo of himself as a toddler!

Mark
January 23, 1986

Like · Comment   👍 2

1984

Mark was born on May
In Dobbs Ferry, New York

Mark's generation was the first to grow up with home computers. Mark used the family computer to create games. His father taught him to write **computer code** and paid a tutor to teach him more.

Mark's coding skills allowed him to program computer versions of well-known board games. At the age of 12, he built a web-based household communication system he called Zucknet. It was similar to instant messaging—before there was instant messaging! It was a small sign of what the budding programming genius could do.

Steve Jobs and the personal computer

In 1976, 23-year-old Steve Jobs cofounded Apple Computer. Apple was immediately involved in efforts to build an easy-to-use home computer. Jobs' first success came in the late 1970s, when the company introduced the Apple II. In 1984, the year that Zuckerberg was born, Apple introduced the Macintosh. Its mouse and on-screen icons set the standard for home computers. Jobs would lead Apple in creating many new products until his death in 2011.

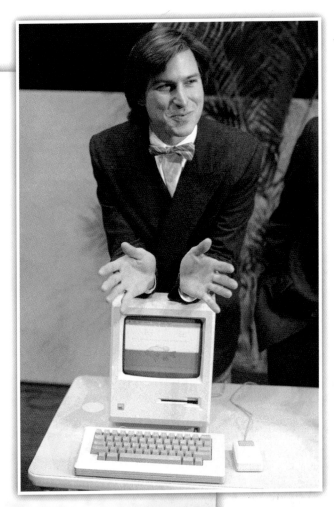

A serious student

As a teenager, Mark had many interests that he took seriously. He transferred from his local high school to Phillips Exeter Academy in New Hampshire. He wanted more challenging classes in computer science, math, and Latin. Exeter is an expensive private school, designed to prepare students for the best universities.

At Exeter, Mark's main focuses were ancient history and languages. By the time he graduated, he had won many academic prizes and could read not just Latin, but also ancient Greek, French, and Hebrew. He was also a **fencing** champion and the team captain. Mark wasn't an average schoolboy!

Students at Phillips Exeter Academy were prepared for the best colleges and universities.

On his college application, Mark Zuckerberg wrote that there were few things he enjoyed more than a good fencing match.

Music for you

While planning a project at Exeter, Mark listened as his computer played a list of songs he liked. Suddenly, the music stopped. All the songs on his list had been played. That gave Mark an idea for his project. Why not create a computer program that would recommend new songs for people, based on what they like?

Mark and a friend built a program that did just that. They called it Synapse. Major companies such as AOL and Microsoft learned about Synapse. They saw that it could be commercially successful and offered more than $1 million for it. The boys' school project could make them rich! But they decided to go to college instead. They also lost interest in Synapse. Soon, similar products were on the market.

"Some companies offered us...up to one million. Then we got another offer that was like two million."
Twenty-year-old Mark Zuckerberg talking about Synapse

Off to Harvard

Mark Zuckerberg entered Harvard University in 2002. One of his majors was computer science. A second was **psychology**. He chose psychology because he was interested in how people thought and got along. The influence of both of his parents clearly showed in his choices.

Zuckerberg was like most students. He studied hard and, at times, played hard. He quickly earned a reputation as a creative computer **programmer**. He had earned money programming in the summer before starting at Harvard. He also occasionally took programming jobs during the school year. Harvard was full of other bright students who often did the same thing.

In his sophomore (second) year, Zuckerberg shared housing with a group of students, including Dustin Moskovitz and Chris Hughes. Their cluttered rooms featured an 8-foot- (2.5-meter-) long classroom whiteboard. The board—and much of the clutter—belonged to Zuckerberg. He used the board to map out his latest ideas.

Could you be a computer programmer?

Every computer has two systems: **hardware** and **software**. Hardware is the electronic and mechanical stuff you can touch inside the computer. Software refers to the programs—or systems—that tell the hardware or other software what to do.

People who create software are computer programmers. They are also known as code writers because they use computer languages or code to write programs. To become programmers, people need to be able to think logically, creatively, and visually; to pay attention to detail; to have patience; to learn complicated computer code languages; and to type well. Could you do it?

Mark Zuckerberg and Chris Hughes work outdoors at Harvard. They were students and entrepreneurs.

Programming for fun

Even as a busy student, Zuckerberg had frequent programming "all-nighters." He coded software programs. Often, his creations helped him with his studies. He shared these with some of the other students.

Some of Zuckerberg's programs had a social theme. They were built around how students related to each other and the existing **social networks** in Harvard. For example, Zuckerberg created Course Match, a website that helped Harvard students choose classes based on who else was in the class.

Harvard University has a tradition of producing successful students in many subjects.

One programming adventure got him into trouble. It was called Facemash. It invited students to compare official photos of classmates to decide who was "hot or not." To get the photos, Zuckerberg spent a night **hacking** into university computers. Once the Facemash website was running, Harvard students flocked to it. Then the university found out about the site and closed it down immediately. The site only existed for several hours, but it earned Zuckerberg a reputation among students as a serious programmer. It also earned him **probation**.

Making friends: social networking before Mark Zuckerberg

A social network is a group of people tied together by common circumstances or interests, such as a school or a hobby. Before Facebook, there were other web-based companies built to create social networks. These websites included Friendster, MySpace, and LinkedIn. Each site built networks in different ways and for different purposes.

Before the web sites existed, people created their own networks—and still do. For example, sending out the same e-mail to a group of friends is a form of social networking. Instant messaging is another example.

The theme is connecting

Although building Facemash was a stupid prank, it led to positive things for Zuckerberg. Perhaps out of guilt, he used his programming skills to help other Harvard students create their own campus websites. Students who hoped to develop profitable online sites also sought him out.

At both Phillips Exeter Academy and Harvard, Mark Zuckerberg was interested in social networking.

One group of students was working on an idea called the Harvard Connection. It was a website that would direct students to social gatherings. The students were Divya Narendra and twin brothers Tyler and Cameron Winklevoss. They paid Zuckerberg to write code for their site.

Social networking

Some people claim that Zuckerberg stole Harvard Connection ideas while working for the site. Yet in all of Zuckerberg's programming projects, there was often a common theme: how people connect to each other directly or through other friends— in other words, social networking. Since his school days at Exeter, Zuckerberg had thought about how to do this with an effective website. He and the friend who created Synapse had even talked about a social networking idea before they went to college.

During the winter break in his sophomore year, Zuckerberg again spent nights and days in front of a computer screen. In early January 2004, he paid $35 to officially register a web address for his planned site. He called it Thefacebook.com.

"I was a psychology major at the same time as being a computer-science major. I was always interested in how these two things combined."

Mark Zuckerberg in *Time* Magazine, 2010

Thefacebook.com launches

On February 4, 2004, Zuckerberg launched Thefacebook.com on the Harvard campus. Within three weeks of going online, Thefacebook.com (renamed Facebook 18 months later) had more than 6,000 Harvard students and **alumni** users.

Word about the new website spread. Days after it launched, students from other universities were asking to join Facebook, too. Zuckerberg saw that Facebook might be a success of some sort. In March, he expanded it to four other **elite** universities in the United States. In each one, Facebook grew quickly in popularity. That spring, Zuckerberg also formed a business partnership with Dustin Moskovitz, Chris Hughes, and another friend, Eduardo Saverin. Their goal was to make Facebook a business. Today, all four are wealthy young men.

Mark Zuckerberg's idea

The idea behind Facebook was different from other social network sites. Those sites pulled people together for specific reasons, such as dating, game playing, or finding jobs. Facebook was simpler. It was a place where people could interact with each other for any reason. Zuckerberg knew that people would determine their own reasons for using it.

Facebook was also different in another way. On other social network sites, members could use made-up names and false photos. Facebook users had to post their real names and real faces, just like old-fashioned university facebooks. Zuckerberg understood that people would use Facebook to really get to know each other.

Zuckerberg's programming ability made the site user friendly. But it was his understanding of human psychology that made the site *friend* friendly. The combination of his two interests—programming and psychology—made Facebook unique.

"I assume eventually I'll make something that is profitable."

Mark Zuckerberg, quoted in the Harvard University student newspaper several weeks after he launched Thefacebook.com

Facebook has changed a lot since it was first introduced in 2004.

The Summer Vacation That Never Ended

In mid-May 2004, Mark Zuckerberg turned 20. That same month, Facebook reached 100,000 users. This early success suggested that Facebook might grow much larger. For that to happen, Zuckerberg needed to raise money. Running and expanding Facebook wasn't cheap. As one source of cash, Zuckerberg reluctantly agreed to accept some advertisements on Facebook.

Facebook wasn't the only programming project that Zuckerberg was trying to create. He was especially interested in developing new software he called Wirehog. It would allow users to share files with each other. Zuckerberg was working on it with Andrew McCallum. McCallum was Zuckerberg's friend from Exeter. It was McCallum who helped him create Synapse.

To develop all of his projects, Zuckerberg moved the business to Palo Alto in California's Silicon Valley for the summer. He rented a small house that served as Facebook's office. It was also a home to Zuckerberg and his coworkers, some of whom he hired in Silicon Valley. One of those was Sean Parker, who was to become a great influence on Facebook's future.

That June, most students went back home for the summer, but not Zuckerberg. He packed a load of computer gear and headed west to start the summer vacation of a lifetime.

"I mean it was never this big decision where it's like, 'Okay, at this point, I am going to drop out of school and then I'm gonna start a company and its gonna be this crazy thing.' It just happened very gradually and at each step, we were just, kind of, doing what made sense to do next."

Mark Zuckerberg talking about how Facebook became such a big company

Silicon Valley: home sweet home

Silicon Valley, an area south of San Francisco, is home to computer and electronic companies such as Hewlett-Packard, Apple, Google, and Yahoo. This unofficial name developed because **silicon** is used to make electronic circuits. Stanford University, near Palo Alto, is home to a research center that has developed many electronic **innovations**. New technology companies such as Facebook often start up in Silicon Valley because some of the world's best computer scientists and programmers study and work there.

Work, work, fun, work

The Palo Alto house was like a very messy students' clubhouse. Yet it had some rules. When programmers worked long hours on computers that filled the dining room, silence ruled. The programmers even used instant messaging to communicate with each other in the same room rather than talk! Zuckerberg was a firm boss who insisted no play was allowed until work was done.

Of course, play was important. The house had an outdoor pool and became the center of loud, late-night parties. The house also suffered a lot of accidental damage. When the owner came to check on the property, he was angry. Zuckerberg had to find a second Silicon Valley home/office/clubhouse—which soon looked like the first!

Sean Parker lived with the other Facebookers. He already had online company successes and offered Zuckerberg guidance. But he wanted Zuckerberg to drop his other projects. Zuckerberg refused. Still, by the end of the summer, Parker was president of Facebook. Zuckerberg was **chief executive officer (CEO)**, and always the boss.

Sean Parker developed Napster, a web site that changed how music was sold.

Sean Parker, web entrepreneur

Sean Parker was seven when his father taught him programming. When he was 16, Parker hacked into U.S. military and business computers. He was arrested, but he didn't go to prison because he was so young. As a young adult, Parker helped develop Napster, an online music-sharing service. Napster angered the music industry because it allowed users to download music files without paying for them. In 2002, Parker cofounded Plaxo, another social networking service. Parker has a reputation for knowing which Internet businesses will work and how to get money to help them grow.

Getting serious

Zuckerberg and his partners had been spending their own money to develop Facebook. They needed much more to keep growing. That's when Parker's experience really became important. He successfully got $500,000 from Peter Thiel, a wealthy **venture capitalist** who helped new companies.

Thiel's support meant a lot. He already had early success in Internet businesses. He had cofounded Paypal, a company that helps people safely pay for products and services bought over the Internet. The company made him very rich. He then expanded his wealth by becoming a venture capitalist. His intelligence and experience made him a wise investor. His investment in Facebook proved that once again. It also told other people that Facebook might have a good future.

Good and bad news

In autumn 2004, Zuckerberg decided not to return to Harvard. He stayed in Silicon Valley. Facebook now had 200,000 users. Two new features were added to Facebook: the Wall and Groups. People could use their Walls to post news, opinions, and more to share with their friends. Groups allowed people to share common interests and ideas.

How do new businesses get money?

New businesses need money for offices, equipment, and more. How do they get it? One way is through **loans**. A loan is borrowed money that has to be paid back with **interest**. Interest is the charge for the loan. Another way of raising money is selling **shares**. Shares give a person part ownership of a company. If the company makes **profits**, that person makes money, too. In 2004, Facebook started using venture capital. That meant that wealthy individuals or investment firms gave Facebook money. Facebook then promised that in the future those people or firms would get shares in Facebook.

Not all the news was good. Zuckerberg's classmates who had hired him to work on the Harvard Connection were still around. After Facebook was launched, they immediately launched their own site, ConnectU. They also claimed that Zuckerberg stole their codes. In September 2004, ConnectU filed a **lawsuit** against Zuckerberg. It was the beginning of a long, expensive battle.

Facebook's Growing Challenges

By the beginning of 2005, Facebook had one million users. Zuckerberg also had two constant problems. Too many people wanted to become Facebook friends, and too many large **corporations** wanted to buy his company.

Zuckerberg knew that the Facebook **servers** weren't ready to handle more people. Having too many visitors can crash a website. If that happens too often, it can crash a business. This problem was solved in May 2005, when Parker arranged to get $12.7 million from a venture capital firm called Accel Partners. Facebook bought more servers. Now it could allow high school students to join Facebook.

By this time, many corporations were interested in buying Facebook. But this was nothing new. The first offer (for $10 million) came only four months after Facebook started. In 2005, MySpace, another social networking website, was sold to a large company for $580 million. But Zuckerberg wasn't interested in selling Facebook. Over the years, offers have kept coming. The highest so far has been $15 billion.

Servers cost money

When Facebook was launched, Mark Zuckerberg paid $85 to rent space on a web server. A web server is a computer that stores **databases** and programs. The more databases and programs a website has, the more server space it needs. Within weeks, Zuckerberg was paying $450 per month for five servers. During the first month in Palo Alto, he spent $20,000 on buying servers. After that, Zuckerberg only added new users on Facebook when there was enough server space. In 2010, Facebook spent $50 million on servers. That's a lot of money—and users.

Servers like this not only store Facebook information, they are connected with other servers, which are connected with other servers, and so on. Together, they make up the Internet.

Facebook figures, photos ... and fun

Money from Accel Partners in 2005 helped Zuckerberg to expand Facebook. The year was significant in other ways, too. Until August 2005, the company's legal name was still Thefacebook.com. Zuckerberg now officially changed it to just Facebook. Later in the year, new Facebook friends were accepted from international schools. Facebook was now global.

As 2005 ended, the number of users hit 5.5 million. New servers also allowed Facebook to add a Photos section to their pages. Before that, only one photo per user was allowed. Now there could be unlimited numbers. Today, billions of users' photos are stored on Facebook servers.

The Photos section decision wasn't easy for Zuckerberg. He worried about cluttering up the site. Yet Zuckerberg listened to his partners and recognized the value that photos would add. The photos could be tagged with users' names, showing who was in them. That helped make Facebook the social site Zuckerberg wanted it to be.

Mark Zuckerberg's hidden humor

In Facebook's early days, when users searched for names of people they knew, a small box appeared at the bottom of the search results. In it were odd quotes, such as "Too close for missiles. Switching to guns." Students around the country debated about what the quotes meant. The answer was easier than they thought. They were lines from films that Mark Zuckerberg liked, or liked to make fun of. The line above is from the film *Top Gun*.

Facebook's first office

Another social site was Facebook's first real office. It was located over a Chinese restaurant and cheerfully decorated with art created by Facebook staff and friends. Outside the office was a large, old, wooden sign in the shape of a chef. At one time, it showed a restaurant menu. Zuckerberg put Facebook "help wanted" advertisements on it!

As offbeat as the office was, some very rich people visited it. They were people Zuckerberg was happy to see: more venture capitalists. They may or may not have been impressed by the office, but they were impressed by Zuckerberg and Facebook. In early 2006, a group invested more than $27 million in the two-year-old company. That was a lot of trust to put into a 21-year-old's hands.

One of Facebook's first employees, Mark Cohler, worked with Mark Zuckerberg in the office over the Chinese restaurant.

A hectic time

Life at Facebook was both relaxed and hectic at the same time—like Zuckerberg himself. He was low-key about his personal life, but intense about his work. Zuckerberg still wore T-shirts and sandals, just as he had at Harvard. He worked wherever there was a space, even if that meant sitting on the office floor. Even though he was wealthy, Zuckerberg lived simply. He didn't buy large houses or fast cars.

In the autumn of 2006, Facebook was only 30 months old. Zuckerberg had to decide whether to open Facebook membership to everyone, not just school and university students. Some Facebookers thought this was a bad idea. Would young people want their parents on Facebook? Would the fact that anyone could join make Facebook "uncool?" Zuckerberg thought it over carefully, then said, "Let's do it." His real goal was to connect the world on the pages of Facebook.

Facebook's growth

It was a smart decision. By the end of the year, there were 10 million active Facebook friends. Facebook's success made it even more valuable. Many more companies wanted to buy Facebook, and more of Zuckerberg's coworkers wanted to sell it.

Wealthy corporations sent a long stream of people to talk to Zuckerberg. His days and evenings were filled with meetings. Most of the corporations could see the great, growing value of Facebook. This meant Zuckerberg received offers of huge sums of money to sell the company.

"Almost any mistake you can make in running a company, I've probably made."

Mark Zuckerberg in a 2010 *Time* magazine interview

Zuckerberg's partners and employees often knew about the offers. They knew they would probably benefit from the sale. Some Facebook people could become rich. Did his partners and employees hope Zuckerberg would sell the company?

Zuckerberg seemed unsure at times about what he really wanted to do. He was under great stress. His health suffered. He often fainted. At the age of 22, he had the unexpected weight of Facebook on his shoulders. He was founder and CEO of one the world's fastest-growing companies. It was a tough job for someone so young.

The rapid success of Facebook forced Zuckerberg into some difficult decisions. This placed a lot of pressure on his young shoulders.

Zuckerberg's Changing Role

Mark Zuckerberg gradually grew into his CEO job. He stopped programming—something he loved—and focused on running the company. He worked to make Facebook "a social **utility** that helps people communicate more efficiently with their friends, family, and coworkers."

Zuckerberg also made Facebook a **platform** for other companies to use. A platform is a system on which computer programs run. Facebook Platform allows anyone to create programs to use on Facebook—for example, games, video tours, and advertisements. Companies share their programs with Facebook's millions of friends. Platform is free, and Facebook allows companies to earn money using the programs they create. That was Zuckerberg's idea. When Facebook Platform launched in 2007, people thought it was crazy to give it away, but Zuckerberg knew Facebook would benefit. It would become a utility for businesses. He was right.

CityVille is one of the games built on the Facebook Platform.

Facebook, like electricity and other utilities, is everywhere.

How does Facebook make money?

Facebook earns money by selling advertising space to companies. At first, Zuckerberg didn't want many ads on Facebook. He thought they would interfere with social networking. So Facebook only sold enough ads to pay for expenses. Eventually, Facebook decided to sell more ads, but Zuckerberg kept them small. They're still small—but they're effective.

Some ads are randomly placed on users' pages. Others target users' interests. If Facebook users talk about something they like, they may later see ads on their pages for it. Facebook Platform gives Facebook more places to put ads.

Facebook earns money through deals with other companies. For example, Microsoft pays Facebook a lot of money for placing its Bing search engine on search lists.

Changing faces

As Facebook grew, it needed different kinds of talent. Sean Parker helped to bring venture capital to the new company. In 2008, Sheryl Sandberg became **chief operating officer (COO)**. She made the company more profitable. In many ways, she caused a change in Zuckerberg's approach. From the beginning, he was concerned about Facebook quality and its user growth. Now, he's also focused on its **bottom line**—money.

What does Facebook know about you?

Facebook encourages openness. Facebook friends use real names and share personal information. Not surprisingly, people sometimes worry about what happens to that information. From the beginning, Zuckerberg allowed users to control what they share, but it can be hard to understand those controls. Occasionally, personal information has spilled out. Since 2007, people have worried even more about privacy, as Facebook introduced new features that seemed to reveal more about them.

Soon, one billion people around the world will regularly use Facebook. Not all of these people will be good. Some will try to use other people's personal information in bad ways. Privacy experts warn all social media users to be careful.

What Facebook shares

Facebook shares what it knows about users with advertisers. It will not give advertisers the names of people who like, for example, skateboarding. However, it will send a skateboard company's ads to the Facebook pages of users who are skateboard fans. Although other websites also do this, Facebook and Zuckerberg seem to get more criticism for it.

Sheryl Sandberg, chief operating officer

Sheryl Sandberg grew up near Miami, Florida. One of her first jobs was teaching aerobics as a high school student. In 2008, she became Facebook's second in command. She oversees the company's business operations. Sandberg graduated from Harvard University with highest honors. While working on a project at Harvard, Sandberg put so much data on university computers that she crashed the system. About ten years later, another Harvard student achieved the same result. That student was Mark Zuckerberg.

Zuckerberg's legal troubles

Success has brought Zuckerberg legal challenges. The Harvard classmates who founded ConnectU first filed a lawsuit against him when he was just 20 years old. That was settled four years later. It cost Facebook $65 million. The beginning of that dispute was the subject of a film called *The Social Network*.

Other people have also filed lawsuits against Zuckerberg, claiming pieces of Facebook. Lawsuits are now a permanent part of Zuckerberg's life. It is an unexpected cost of starting a successful company.

Many people incorrectly assume they know the real Mark Zuckerberg because of the film *The Social Network*.

On the television program *Saturday Night Live*, Mark Zuckerberg (left) met Jesse Eisenberg (center), the actor who played him in *The Social Network*. On the right is Andy Samberg, a comedian who poked fun at Zuckerberg on television.

The film ... and the man

So, what happens when a 19 year old starts a business and soon becomes the youngest self-made billionaire in history? Someone makes a film about him! In 2010, the story of Zuckerberg's fantastic launch of Facebook was told in the film *The Social Network*, based on the book *The Accidental Billionaires*. The film was very popular and won many awards. But it was a fictional story based on Zuckerberg's Harvard days. It showed him as awkward, scheming, and dishonest. The film's producers admitted that they changed the truth to tell a more interesting story. The Zuckerberg in the film isn't the real Zuckerberg. Yet he is the only Zuckerberg that millions of filmgoers know.

Mark Zuckerberg Today

In 2010, *Time* magazine named Zuckerberg the Person of the Year. The magazine chose him because of his leadership, success, and vision for the future of social networking.

The number of people who actively use Facebook hit 845 million by the end of 2011. In the summer of that year, Zuckerberg also announced that Facebook friends could talk to and see each other live. This is another effort to make Facebook a social utility. It's likely that music and film programs will be added to Facebook. It's no surprise that online competitors are looking for ways to challenge Facebook's growth.

Rewards and challenges

Zuckerberg has profited well from his efforts. In 2011, a U.S. magazine called *Forbes* estimated his personal fortune to be near $17 billion—but he has yet to spend much of this on himself. After years of renting modest houses in Palo Alto in California, he finally bought a mansion for $7 million. That is a lot of money to spend on a house, but by billionaire standards it is still modest.

Facebook's business rivals

Like all businesses, Facebook faces competition from other companies. Some comes from companies that specialize in social networking. The strongest competitor was MySpace, but in 2008, Facebook easily passed it in popularity. Sean Parker said that the MySpace website just wasn't as easy to use or as fast as Facebook's.

Other social networking companies are Twitter, LinkedIn, Bebo (in the United Kingdom), and QQ (in China). Competition also comes from bigger internet companies, such as Google and Yahoo. Some people consider these companies to be social utilities. In 2011, Google launched a social network of its own called Google+.

When he was voted *Time* magazine's Person of the Year for 2010, Zuckerberg was just 26 years old.

Life as a billionaire

Zuckerberg has always said that wealth wasn't as important to him as Facebook itself and the worldwide social network it represents. He has proved that by pledging to give much of his money away. Like Microsoft's Bill Gates and other wealthy entrepreneurs, Zuckerberg has pledged to donate a large part of his fortune—as much as half—to various charitable causes.

In 2010, he donated $100 million to improve the school system in Newark, New Jersey. Some critics, fairly or not, have said the donation was to erase the bad publicity that Zuckerberg received from *The Social Network* film.

Life will never be simple for Zuckerberg. Facebook is now used in 190 countries, but it is also banned in some. In some countries, people don't like what users say on Facebook, and they blame Zuckerberg. That is similar to blaming the phone company because you don't like what someone said to you on the phone. There are rumors that Zuckerberg's life has even been threatened because of how Facebook has been used.

From a few students in late winter 2004, to more than 750 million people in summer 2011, the growth in active Facebook users has been phenomenal.

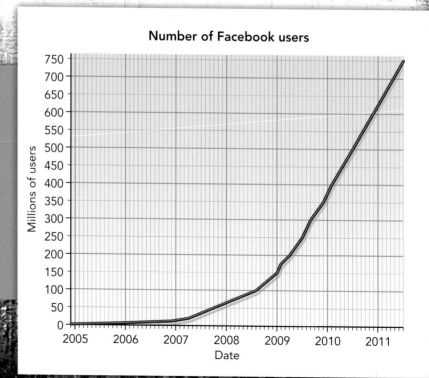

Number of Facebook users

Complaints

A less threatening criticism of Zuckerberg comes from some of Facebook's active users. Facebook changes constantly. Zuckerberg's programmers hunt for and find better ways to do things. Zuckerberg often introduces inventive extras for users. Recent new features include Questions and Timeline.

However, each introduction or change brings complaints from some users. There are even Facebook groups that exist just to complain about Facebook changes. These users like Facebook's "old ways." Zuckerberg must smile. How can a company that is so young and run by people so young really have old ways?

Mayor Cory Booker of Newark, New Jersey, Governor Chris Christie, and Mark Zuckerberg are discussing improvements to the school system in Newark. Zuckerberg donated millions of dollars to help.

The Zuckerberg Effect

Facebook is fast approaching one billion active users. That's almost one in every seven people on Earth. When Mark Zuckerberg launched Thefacebook.com, could he have known that it would grow that big? It seems impossible.

> "Sometimes you have to admit that winners can see the future far before the rest of us. They might zig or zag on the way, but they have a clear idea of who they are, what they're doing, and where they want to head."
>
> Liz Gannes, writing about Mark Zuckerberg on gigaom.com

Winner takes all

Winners take a lot of people with them. With Facebook, it's not just the users. The new Facebook headquarters is the size of a university campus, with room for 9,000 employees. That's four or five times more than those who work there now.

Most of the people in Zuckerberg's company earn good livings. Some may earn a lot more when Facebook shares are sold to the public in 2012. The company is estimated to be worth $75–100 billion. Some individuals and companies that have used Facebook Platform to create their own businesses have also profited. Other companies have seen their businesses expand thanks to their use of advertisements on Facebook pages.

Zuckerberg knew about the wealth that successful entrepreneurs could create. But that isn't why he founded Facebook. He simply wanted to give people a place to share information and a photo. Some have shared much more than that. They've shared the wealth that Mark Zuckerberg created.

"I'm trying to make the world a more open place by helping people connect and share."

Mark Zuckerberg, on his Facebook page

Mark Zuckerberg is already a successful and wealthy man. Who knows what the future holds for him?

How to Become an Entrepreneur

Can you be the next Mark Zuckerberg? Well, few people will be as successful as he has been. Yet Zuckerberg did some things that you can also do to help you reach your dreams.

Develop your interests

Zuckerberg learned programming because he liked computers. He learned Latin and ancient Greek because he liked history. He studied psychology because he was curious about people. He didn't know that any of those things would make him rich. They just interested him.

Do what you most enjoy

Zuckerberg says that if he hadn't loved computer programming, he would not have had the determination to do the work needed to create Facebook.

Understand your strengths and where they can take you

Zuckerberg was a fencing champ, but he probably didn't have the talent to go to the Olympics. He also had incredible programming skills. He judged correctly that it would be the programming skills that would lead him to success.

Imagine what can happen

More than most teenagers, Zuckerberg looked ahead and thought about what could happen. Somehow he imagined a world united by a website—a website that he could develop. He wasn't afraid of what he imagined. He acted on it.

Is college a good idea?

Mark Zuckerberg is a billionaire, but he didn't graduate from college. However, over their lifetimes, college graduates earn about 77 percent more money than people who don't go to college. Even those who attend college but don't graduate earn more on average than people who go to work straight from school. Zuckerberg met students at Harvard, shared ideas with them, invented Facebook, and became business partners with a few of them. Plus, when Facebook started to grow, he hired college graduates.

Mark Zuckerberg first connected with college students, and then the world.

Glossary

alumni graduates of a school, college, or university

bottom line amount of money that a company makes or loses over a set period of time

chief executive officer (CEO) highest-ranking person in a company; the boss

chief operating officer (COO) high-ranking person in a company. The COO often runs the day-to-day business.

computer code language used to tell a computer how to do something

corporation company that can legally make and sell products

database part of a computer system where information is organized and stored

directory book that lists the names, addresses, and phone numbers of a collection of individuals

elite superior or highest-performing members within a group

fencing sport of fighting with thin swords

hacking often illegal act of using computer skills to enter and search someone's computer, or to change a computer program or website

hardware physical parts of a computer

innovation new way of doing or making something

interest money that is charged by banks, companies, or individuals when they lend money to people. The interest is usually a percentage of the amount of money loaned.

lawsuit legal accusation of wrongdoing made against somebody. The argument is often settled in court or through other legal means.

loan amount of money lent to a person or company. The borrower must pay back the money, plus interest.

platform computer system on which other systems or programs can be built

probation period of supervision for a person convicted of a wrongdoing or crime

profit financial gain made from a business or investment

programmer person who writes computer programs or code

psychology the study of the mind and the ways that people feel and act

server large computer that stores large amounts of information and data

share single, small part of ownership in a company. Each share is equal in value to other shares in the company.

silicon chemical that occurs naturally in the earth and that is often used in producing computer-related parts

social network group of people who communicate and interact with each other about at least one common interest

software data programs that can be run on a computer. Software can be games, word processing programs, media players, and so on.

utility public service. The most common utilities are gas, electricity, and water.

venture capital money invested in a new company by an individual, a business, or a group of people. The investment is often risky, but there is a chance to make great profits.

Find Out More

Books

Lusted, Marcia Amidon. *Social Networking: MySpace, Facebook, and Twitter* (Technology Pioneers). San Francisco, Calif.: Essential Library, 2011.

Maida, Jerome, and Fritz Saalfeld. *Mark Zuckerberg: Creator of Facebook GN*. Vancouver, Wash.: Bluewater Productions, 2012.

Ryan, Peter K. *Social Networking* (Digital and Information Literacy). New York: Rosen, 2011.

Sutherland, Adam. *The Story of Facebook* (The Business of High Tech). New York: Rosen, 2012.

Williams, Gabrielle J. *The Making of a Young Entrepreneur: A Kid's Guide to Developing the Mind-Set for Success*. Bowie, Md.: Legacy Builder Group, 2011.

Woog, Adam. *Mark Zuckerberg: Facebook Creator* (Innovators). San Diego, Calif.: KidHaven Press, 2010.

Websites

archive.sba.gov/teens

If you're an aspiring young entrepreneur, check out this "Teen Business Link" website of the U.S. Small Business Administration to get some tips and ideas.

ecorner.stanford.edu/author/mark_zuckerberg

This series of videos show Mark Zuckerberg talking about entrepreneurship.

www.facebook.com/zuck

Check out Mark's Facebook page for more info on the man himself and the latest Facebook updates.

www.themint.org/kids/entrepreneur-challenge.html

If you think you might be interested in starting your own business, take the "Entrepreneur Challenge" at this website. Maybe you could be a titan of business someday!

www.time.com/time/specials/packages/
article/0,28804,2036683_2037183_2037185,00.html

This article explains why Mark Zuckerberg was *Time* magazine's Person of the Year in 2010.

Topics to research

After reading the book, what do you find the most interesting about Mark Zuckerberg? What business ideas does reading about his success inspire in you? To learn more, you might want to research the following topics:

- Entrepreneurship for young people
- Social networking websites
- Silicon Valley
- Sean Parker, Sheryl Sandberg
- Web companies such as Google, Yahoo, and AOL

You can visit your local library to learn more about any of these fascinating subjects.

Index